Japanese Politics
One Politician's Perspective

From the DPJ administration to the LDP-KOMEITO ruling coalition
(2010-2019)

Yuzuru TAKEUCHI

文芸社

Introduction 7

Chapter I

The Democratic Party of Japan Administration

The instability of the DPJ Government 11
Why do Prime Ministers in Japan change so quickly? 13
What is the DPJ's Economic Policy? 15
The cause of Deflation in Japan. 17
Undesirable Competitive Devaluation of Currencies 19
Diplomatic challenges with China and the DPJ Government 21
Immature Diplomacy of the DPJ Government 23
The Failure of the DPJ's Foreign Policies 25
The North Korean Military Crisis 27
What should the DPJ Administration do?
~ Complete Solution for the North Korea Abduction Issue! 29
Can the Fiscal 2011 Budget be passed in the Diet? 31
Where is the Non Bureaucratic led Government the DPJ promised ? 33
The Destiny of the DPJ 35
The Effects of the Great East Japan Earthquake 37
Political Circumstances after the Earthquake 39
When will Prime Minister Naoto Kan resign? 42
Why has the DPJ Administration failed? 44
Should Japan stop Nuclear Power Generation? 46
From Two Party Politics to a Three Party Era 48
The Trans Pacific Partnership (TPP) 50

The Beginning of the End for the DPJ Administration 52
The Reason the KOMEITO agreed to the Consumption Tax hike 53
How can Japan overcome Deflation? 55
Can the LDP take back Power? 57

Chapter II

The Liberal Democratic Party / The KOMEITO Ruling Coalition

The Start of the Second LDP and KOMEITO Ruling Coalition 61
What is "Abenomics"? 63
The Political Relevance of the 2013 Upper House Election 65
Consumption tax hike and reduced tax rate 67
A visit to India 71
Can a Cabinet reinterpret Article 9 of the Constitution? 73
Should Japan reduce the corporate tax rate? 76
Cabinet decision on the right of Collective Self-Defense to ensure
Japan's survival and protect its people 78
The LDP and KOMEITO retain a ruling coalition 80
Security Legislations are Constitutional 82
My hopes as the State Minister of Health, Labor and Welfare 84
Right wing and Centrist Line VS. Left wing and Communist Line 86
An Era of Division and Conflict 89
A Turning Point for the Abe Administration 92
The House of Representatives General Election 2017 94
The Mission of the KOMEITO in the Abe Administration 97

How to stabilize a deteriorating global political environment 100

Can Human Race control Global Warming? 102

The Importance of the KOMEITO as a Centrist Party 105

The Relationship between the KOMEITO and China 108

Should we consider Modern Monetary Theory (MMT)? 111

Japan should put more emphasis on Basic Scientific Research 115

Bitter dispute between Japan and South Korea,
and Hong Kong Issue 117

Chapter III
The History of the KOMEITO

The History of the KOMEITO 123

Two election defeats made me grow as a statesman 126

Profile "Yuzuru TAKEUCHI" 2019 129

The National Diet Building

Introduction

This work consists of a series of blogs I wrote regarding political themes with an emphasis on the now defunct Democratic Party of Japan (DPJ) administration (2009-2012) and the Liberal Democratic Party (LDP) / the KOMEITO ruling coalition (2013-2019). Why did I write these blogs in English instead of Japanese?

In September 2010, I went to Hong Kong government as a delegation member of the KOMEITO. The government officials welcomed us heartily and explained their political, administrative and economic circumstances for Hong Kong. They were also very much interested in Japanese politics and put many questions to me. One question, in particular, why did the Prime Minister of Japan change so quickly? This was a hard question for me to explain precisely in English. I fully realized the importance of explaining the political circumstances of Japan and our viewpoints to international society.

Currently, divisions and conflicts amongst people have deepened in the advanced nations, while only Japan has been relatively stable since the second Abe administration which started in 2013. The Abe administration has been gaining attention from international society. How has Prime Minister Abe retained his administration for such a long time? In order to answer this question, I have analyzed the LDP-KOMEITO ruling coalition to explain the role of the KOMEITO in this book.

These blogs were written chronologically from 2010 to 2019, which will vividly remind readers of the various issues and agendas at that time. Therefore, this book may be viewed as a historical document, and could be used as a reference for high school and university students with an interest in Japanese politics.

The contents of this book are my views regarding Japanese politics, and do not necessarily express the thoughts and official policies of the KOMEITO party.

I would like to express my profound gratitude to Mr. Jason Tonge who proofread my manuscripts and advised me through discussion for the last decade.

Members of the Hong Kong Legislative Council.
Yuzuru TAKEUCHI, third from the left.

Chapter I

The Democratic Party of Japan Administration

The DPJ won a landslide victory in the 2009 House of Representatives election with huge expectations from people, which was the first change of administration since the introduction of the single seat electoral system in 1994. This was a historical event for Japanese politics.

Nevertheless, soon after, the DPJ administration fell into dysfunction due to repeated misjudgments and conflicts between its own factions. Japanese politics was thrown into confusion and, as a result, the DPJ administration finally collapsed in December 2012.

Why did the DPJ administration fail so quickly? I analyzed the cause from various viewpoints, such as the quality of prime ministers, party governance, economic and foreign policies, its "Non Bureaucratic-led Government", and the response to the Great East Japan Earthquake. We can learn valuable lessons from the DPJ's failures.

Plenary session, the House of Representatives, October 2010.

The instability of the DPJ Government
(September 2010)

On August 30 2009, the Democratic Party of Japan (DPJ) won the general election in the House of Representatives. As a result, a historical change of government has been made. The DPJ has come to power and Mr. Hatoyama became the Prime Minister of Japan.

However, in July 2010, Mr. Hatoyama suddenly resigned as the Prime Minister as doubts were raised regarding a large political donation from his mother. At the same time, Mr. Ozawa also resigned as the Secretary General of the DPJ due to accusations surrounding his huge political funds. Subsequently Mr. Naoto Kan took office as the Prime Minister.

The DPJ then lost the election in the House of Councilors in 2010. The main reason was that the Prime Minister Naoto Kan abruptly pronounced a raise in the consumption tax rate without sufficient approval in the DPJ.

Another reason for this loss was that Mr. Hatoyama was unable to negotiate the issue of the American Futenma Base Camp in Okinawa. Right after Mr. Hatoyama took office as Prime Minister, he pledged to relocate the American Futenma Base Camp in Okinawa to outside Japan or at least out of Okinawa Prefecture. However, recently he admitted his failures and that he misjudged this complex situation and apologized to people.

Lastly, many people began to believe that the manifest the DPJ put forward could not be realized easily.

In the House of Councilors, the DPJ could not secure a majority, which meant the DPJ can pass legislation in the House of Representatives, but not through the House of Councilors.

There are 242 seats in the House of Councilors and the DPJ has only 106 members, which forces the DPJ to cooperate with the LDP, the KOMEITO, and others.

This makes the KOMEITO an important party. The KOMEITO has 19 members in the House of Councilors, and if the KOMEITO cooperates with the DPJ, they would have a majority in the House of Councilors. Currently, the Your Party (MINNA NO TO) has only 11 members.

Another important factor is the Ozawa faction. If the Ozawa faction leaves the DPJ, it will collapse and the political environment in Japan will be thrown into confusion.

Budget Committee, the House of Representatives, November 2010.

Why do Prime Ministers in Japan change so quickly?

(October 2010)

Why do Prime Ministers of Japan change so quickly?

Many foreigners often ask me this question. It is true that during the last 20 years, there has been fourteen different people to take office as the Prime Minister of Japan, and the average term has only been 18 months.

This is a problem that we have to think about seriously.

Superficially, there are a few reasons, for example, scandals, health problems, election defeats, gaffes and so forth. But essentially this issue can be analyzed from both poor personnel choices and changes in the political environment.

The most important factor is unsuitable candidates leading to a lower quality of Prime Minster in Japan. Recently it seems that public opinion polls are strongly dictating Japanese politics. Therefore the person who gains popularity through public opinion polls tends to be elected as the Prime Minister of Japan. Modern politics depend too greatly on public opinion polls, which unfortunately does not necessarily correspond to ability or quality.

This change in the political landscape has brought forward the era of two big parties, with the public now requiring dramatic results in politics.

However, these people calling for change don't belong to a specific party. They are called "Mutouha-sou" in Japanese and they change the parties every election according to the political circumstance.

Mutouha-sou affects public opinion polls and are influenced greatly by political TV shows. I think a few of these TV stations have unclear agendas concerning politics and are sometimes doubted of their fairness. Surprisingly, a lot of statesmen in the Diet tend to be unnerved by public opinion polls. When an approval rating for a cabinet is below 30%, voices to change the Prime Minister usually start boiling over from members of the ruling party. This fact applies to both the LDP and DPJ.

Thus the Prime Minister of Japan has changed so frequently.

Budget Committee, the House of Representatives, November 2010.

What is the DPJ's Economic Policy?

(November 2010)

Deflation has been the biggest concern for the Japanese economy in the last 10 years. This trend has depressed the economic growth of Japan and held down the increase in wages. Under deflation, it is extremely difficult to set order for national finance.

Currently, the yen has been rising rapidly and a strong yen is generally unfavorable for Japanese exporters. As Japan is often called an export-led economy, the higher yen has driven down stock prices.

In order to deal with the strong yen and deflation, on October 5 2010, the Bank of Japan (BOJ) decided to return to a zero-interest rate policy for the first time since July 2006, and this rate will be maintained until the end of deflation is in sight.

As a stimulus measure, the BOJ decided to set up a ¥ 5 trillion fund to purchase a wide range of financial assets including; long-term Japanese government bonds, exchange-traded funds (ETF) and real estate investment trust funds(REIT).

As a result to this announcement, the Nikkei average rebounded sharply on the Tokyo Stock Exchange, however this was short lived as the yen against dollar went up to ¥82 from ¥84. The reason for this temporary gain is that the U.S. economy has been showing signs of stagnation and U.S. interest rate is projected to fall ever further.

After all, the Japanese economy still depends greatly on the U.S. and it is important to our economy that the U.S. economy recovers quickly. It is also important to note that neither country should consider protectionism or a cheap-currency policy. It is vital that both the U.S. and Japan expand their domestic demand to create much needed employment opportunities.

That said, it is fair to say that after the change of government, the DPJ has done almost nothing new for economic policies in Japan, and have only continued to implement policies that had been started from the LDP-KOMEITO coalition administration.

The cancellation of the Yamba dam by the DPJ administration.

The cause of Deflation in Japan.

(November 2010)

Why has the Japanese economy been in deflation for the last decade?

It is strange and a serious problem for our economy is the only advanced country in deflation.

Generally, the cause of deflation is analyzed from both the demand side and supply side. According to analysis from demand side, it is said there is a huge shortage of demand compared to the ability of supply, creating a gap between demand and supply.

The amount of the gap is measured at about ¥35 trillion and it is not easy for the government to rectify this gap. Since there are around ¥800 trillion in national bonds, the government can't issue a lot of bonds for public works projects and tax cuts.

Furthermore, monetary easing policies have been proposed by many economists called *Monetarists*. They insist the reason for deflation is a shortage of money and the level of consumer prices is proportionality in the amount of money. As a result, the Bank of Japan (BOJ) decided to take a zero-interest rate policy and set up a ¥35 trillion fund to supply the money market.

In Japan, it is not clear whether monetary easing policies are effective for deflation, but to some extent they seem to be effective for our economy.

From the viewpoint of the supply side, it is said that during the last decade, an influx of cheap products from developing countries leads to lower domestic consumer prices.

Therefore it is indispensable for Japanese enterprises to implement structural reform and rebuild new business models to respond to this new economical environment. Innovation is required to overcome deflation in Japan.

The Tokyo Stock Exchange. Yuzuru TAKEUCHI, second from the left. Natsuo YAMAGUCHI, Chief Representative of the KOMEITO, center.

Undesirable Competitive Devaluation of Currencies
(November 2010)

On October 22 - 23, 2010, the G20 meeting of Finance Ministers and Central Bank Governors of 20 countries was held in South Korea. The purpose of this conference was to refrain from the competitive devaluation of major currencies and to reduce the excessive trade imbalances, maintaining current account imbalances at sustainable levels.

However competitive devaluation of currencies began with the U.S. dollar while other countries followed suit, taking cheap currency policies to defend their domestic economies.

Since the U.S. economy has worsened recently, the U.S. government wants to expand their exportation two-fold within the next 5 years, acknowledging the falling U.S. dollar.

I think the U.S. government should not take this money easing recovery policy but instead to pursue a structural reform to create much needed employment opportunities. Of course, it is difficult for the U.S. to do so; however, the U.S. has a responsibility for the world economy.

On the other hand, it is true that rapidly developing countries like China and South Korea are already pursuing high technologies and are able to produce similar products cheaper than Japan.

In spite of these facts, both the gen and won have depreciated more than their economic fundamentals. As a result, both countries can easily promote their products to the U.S. and Japan, especially China has received significant profits trading with the U.S.

That is why the G20 announced that they will move towards more market determined exchange rate systems that reflect their economic fundamentals.

Budget Committee, the House of Representatives, November 2010.

Diplomatic challenges with China and the DPJ Government

(December 2010)

It is fair to say that after the change in government, policies on foreign affairs led by the DPJ have not necessarily been implemented well. The previous Prime Minister Yukio Hatoyama, who could not relocate the U.S. Futenma military base in Okinawa, resigned due to this failure.

On September 7, 2010, an incident occurred where a Chinese fishing boat collided with Japanese patrol boats off the disputed Senkaku Islands in the East China Sea, resulting in the arrest of the Chinese skipper.

China applied strong pressure on Japan to release the captain and subsequently arrested four Japanese employees on September 20 for entering a military zone in China without permission. The captain was finally freed by the Okinawa district prosecutors office on September 25.

The incident looks as though Japan had bended to China and the Prime Minister Naoto Kan was blamed for this decision, not only by the opposition parties, but also the members of ruling party.

The government insists that the decision was made by the Okinawa district prosecutors office inline with legal procedures. However, the masses including media, complained that Prime Minister Naoto Kan dodged his responsibilities over the incident, which resulted in this issue being solved by bureaucrats instead of the government.

This result brought a big loss to both Japan and China. The KOMEITO and LDP have constructed a good relationship between Japan and China since the 1960's and currently the amount of trade between the two countries is larger than between Japan and the U.S.

However after this incident, the relationship between Japan and China clearly began to deteriorate.

Plenary session, the House of Representatives, December 2010.

Immature Diplomacy of the DPJ Government
(December 2010)

Japan attempted to arrange a meeting with the Chinese Premier Wen Jiabao in Hanoi during the Association of Southeast Asian Nations summit including Japan, China and South Korea (ASEAN +3).

Prime Minister Naoto Kan wanted to ease the strained relations between Japan and China, however, Beijing rejected Japan's offer citing Japan had ruined the atmosphere for bilateral talks.

I don't know if what Beijing said is true, but Japanese Foreign Minister Seiji Maehara reiterated that no territorial dispute exists since the Senkaku Islands are part of Japan.

It was impolite for China to suddenly cancel this formal diplomatic meeting, but if Japan wants to succeed, various kinds of considerations should be made by the Japanese government and Mr. Maehara has to be prudent in his speech. The cancellation of their formal talks was a diplomatic failure for Japan.

It was then reported that Kan and Wen happened to meet for a 10-minute informal conversation, which was nonsense. This shows that it is extremely difficult to repair the relation between Japan and China. Many people in China demonstrated their anger for Japan and most Japanese people have a negative image of China.

The foreign policy of the DPJ is immature and as a result, difficult problems are going to arise for Japan one after another.

Budget Committee, the House of Representatives, December 2010.

The Failure of the DPJ's Foreign Policies
(December 2010)

On November 1, 2010, President Dmitry Medvedev, for the first time as a Russian leader visited the island of Kunashiri, one of the four islands which lie north of Hokkaido.

This news bitterly angered Japan and in the Diet Prime Minister Naoto Kan insisted that the four northern islands are a part of Japan's territory, and so the president's visit there is very regrettable.

Since Soviet troops invaded the four islands at the end of World War 2, Moscow has occupied these islands. The major reason for the occupation is that the islands contain metal deposits such as gold and silver, and had a strategic importance during the Cold War to confront the United States in the Pacific.

In 1956, diplomatic relations were established and the Soviet Union suggested that two of the disputed islands, Shikotan and Habomai, might be returned under a peace treaty. However Japan refused this suggestion and insisted on the return of all four islands.

This time, Medvedev definitely stated that the four islands are Russian territory and the visit was a domestic issue.

Why have China and Russia recently strengthened their territorial insists for the disputed areas?

I suppose the failure in relocating the U.S. Futenma military base in Okinawa weakened the security alliance between Japan and the U.S., which brought these unwanted results. Both countries may have built-up a tacit collaboration against Japan to test the DPJ's ability.

I feel as if the government led by the DPJ has a destiny to provoke trouble on foreign affairs. Foreign policies in Japan have been constructed by many foreign bureaucrats. Without their knowledge or wisdom, politicians cannot normalize relationships between Japan and other nations.

The DPJ tends to exclude the power of bureaucrats, resulting in failure for foreign policies.

Plenary session, the House of Representatives, December 2010.

The North Korean Military Crisis
(December 2010)

On November 23, 2010, North Korea bitterly bombarded a small island near the North Korea mainland, which belongs to South Korea. Two South Korean marines were killed while 15 troops and 3 civilians were injured in the shelling.

The aim of North Korea is to create nuclear weapons as leverage to negotiate with the U.S. and obtain economic support and recognition of the Kim Jong-il regime. However the U.S. has refused negotiations with North Korea since 1994.

The cause of this incident is that the North Korean leader Kim Jong Il is worried about his health and appointed his youngest son, Kim Jong Un six weeks earlier as his successor.

North Korea has been steadily developing nuclear weapons and has carried out repeated nuclear tests. Recently North Korea revealed a new uranium enrichment facility to a visiting American nuclear scientist.

This incident may be construed as a way to restart negotiations between the U.S. and North Korea. If the U.S. ignores this tacit intention, North Korea may escalate and provoke a new attack on Japan. Therefore it is indispensable for Japan to prepare missile defenses against North Korea.

The United Nations Security Council should condemn North Korea and take sanctions against the illegal attack as soon as possible.

South Korea, the U.S. and Japan have to cooperate with each other in order to create stability in the region.

Moreover it is crucially important for China to persuade the North to abandon nuclear weapons and join the international society. China hopes that North Korea will abandon their nuclear weapons but fears that this may result in the collapse of North Korea.

China doesn't want such a result and will continue giving economic support to North Korea. North Korea will also undoubtedly reject abandoning their nuclear weapons program.

Military tension in North East Asia will continue.

Petition from supporters for the abductees taken by North Korea.

What should the DPJ Administration do?
~ Complete Solution for the North Korea Abduction Issue!
(January 2011)

The expectation for change has almost faded away due to a series of diplomatic failures, gaffes by ministers and continuing economic stagnation. The DPJ government may also be starting to feel the reality of government operation.

It is indispensable for the ruling party to have qualities such as high morals, a definite philosophy, strategy, accumulated policies and maturity in organizations. However, extreme confusion remains by their excessive "lip service" and their manifest full of populism.

The most important political issues in Japan at the moment is to rebuild diplomacy and security policies. Second is to promote economic growth and overcome deflation, and the third is to establish a social welfare vision and secure new sources of revenue to correct national finance.

The government needs to decide on their priorities and steadily advance them using strong leadership. Instead, they have to apologize to the people about what they couldn't realize, only to dash peoples' hope and expectations for future.

We should be careful in regards to security for the Korean Peninsula and make North Korea abandon their nuclear weapons and missiles. This includes finding a complete solution for the North Korea abduction issue.

In 1978, Megumi Yokota, a girl of thirteen and a junior high school student, was abducted by North Korea in Niigata Prefecture. At first, the Japanese police couldn't identify the real culprit, but in

1997, Japanese government recognized 10 abductees taken by North Korea (now 17 abductees). This is unprecedented crimes that violated a Japan's sovereignty and human rights.

In 2002, the former Prime Minister Junichro Koizumi of the LDP-KOMEITO ruling coalition, negotiated with Kim John il on this issue and Kim recognized the abductions by North Korea and apologized. However, this resulted in the return of only five abductees to Japan. North Korea claimed the rest of the abductees, including Megumi Yokota, had died. However, their ashes that North Korea provided turned out to be counterfeit by DNA analysis. They must still remain in North Korea.

I am also a chairperson of the North Korea abduction issue commission of the KOMEITO. The resolution of the abduction issue is especially important for Japan and is a prerequisite condition for normalizing relationship between Japan and North Korea. However, it is regrettable that the DPJ administration has done almost nothing in terms of diplomatic negotiation with North Korea.

The national convention, pursuing a complete solution for the North Korea abduction issue, Tokyo, 2019.

Can the Fiscal 2011 Budget be passed in the Diet?

(February 2011)

The DPJ administration has approved a 92.41 trillion yen budget for fiscal 2011. The budget revenue consists of 41 trillion yen in tax income, 7 trillion yen in non tax revenue and 44 trillion yen in government bonds. The biggest problem with this budget is that the government bond issuance exceeds that of tax revenue, which has occurred for two straight years.

According to the Constitution of Japan, the decision for the budget takes place in the Lower House instead of the Upper House. Currently, the DPJ has the majority in the Lower House, but not the Upper House.

Therefore, even if the budget doesn't make it through the Upper House, it will be established. However, if bills related to the budget are denied in the Upper House, the Lower House needs a two-thirds majority in the Lower House for the budget to pass. But the DPJ does not have a two-thirds majority in the Lower House.

The DPJ therefore depends on the KOMEITO to pass bills related to the budget in the Upper House. If the KOMEITO denies the bills, the fiscal 2011 budget cannot be enforced, which will put extraordinary pressure on society.

Prime Minister Naoto Kan may lose his credibility, which may result in the resignation of the entire Cabinet or dissolution of the Lower House.

However, contrarily, if the KOMEITO does agree to the bills, it may be construed that the KOMEITO lent their hands to the DPJ. This would be a disadvantage to the KOMEITO in the unified local elections in April 2011.

It is extremely difficult for the KOMEITO to take any option on this matter.

Inspection for the Maizuru harbor facilities, a major port of Japan. Yuzuru TAKEUCHI, center.

Where is the Non Bureaucratic led Government the DPJ promised ?

(February 2011)

The approval rate of the Kan Cabinet has fallen below 20% which is said to be a dangerous level for maintaining a Cabinet, and the DPJ administration has suffered during this Diet session.

Before the change of government in 2009, the DPJ promised two major proposals in their manifest. First was a non bureaucratic led government, and the other was to create 16.8 trillion yen in revenue for policies such as child compensation by excluding wasteful spending and transformation of the national budget.

At this time, let's look at the former issue. The DPJ insisted that the LDP government was dependent on bureaucrats, and that bureaucratic led governments have been in place since 1955.

As a result, a strange custom had been put into practice that let many executive bureaucrats parachute into high positions in both private and public sectors before reaching their retirement age. This is called "the Amakudari system".

In order to maintain this system, the bureaucrat organizations had to create new institutions which would accept their executives. Moreover, the bureaucratic led government subsidized such institutions and to date, the amount of subsidy is said to be around 12 trillion yen per year.

When the DPJ was still the opposition party, they promised to stop "the Amakudari system" and abolish institutions which accepted bureaucrat executives and to reduce bureaucratic costs by 20%.

These policies are summarized as the non bureaucratic led government. However, so far, the DPJ government has not realized this promise.

Plenary session, the House of Representatives, February 2011.

The Destiny of the DPJ
(March 2011)

Recently, sixteen members of the DPJ expressed interest to leave the DPJ parliamentary group and form another group, but still remain in the party. They are loyal to Ichiro Ozawa and have complaints regarding the Kan Cabinet. As a result, on March 1, they were absent during voting on the fiscal 2011 budget in the plenary session of the House of Representatives.

After this incident, Mr. Matsuki, a parliamentary official from the Ministry of Agriculture, Forestry and Fisheries, resigned for similar reasons. Moreover, Yuko Sato, a member of the House of Representatives, left the DPJ on March 3. These moves show the beginnings of the DPJ collapse.

The budget-related bills will be passed in the House of Representatives, but not the House of Councilors. The KOMEITO has decided to oppose the budget-related bills.

Therefore, if those sixteen members are absent from the second round of voting on budget-related bills in the House of Representatives, the ruling parties will not get the two-thirds majority and the bills won't be established.

The fiscal budget cannot be implemented without the budget-related bills and the Kan Cabinet will lose its credibility.

If the LDP submits a no-confidence motion against Kan's Cabinet, Prime Minister Naoto Kan and his entire Cabinet may have to resign or dissolve the House of Representatives.

In the case of a general election in the near future, the DPJ may be defeated, which could result in the collapse of the DPJ. It's a pity that two-party politics in Japan might culminate in failure so quickly.

Festival at Misonobashi 801 shopping arcade, Kyoto City, 2011.

The Effects of the Great East Japan Earthquake
(April 2011)

On March 11 2011, a massive earthquake rocked the Tohoku region which measured a magnitude of 9.0, the fourth largest in human history. Soon after a huge "tsunami" hit the coast and more than 20 thousand people are thought to have lost their lives.

Moreover, the nuclear power plant in Fukushima prefecture was damaged by the earthquake and tsunami, and a series of serious accidents occurred.

Prime Minister Naoto Kan and the DPJ government must organize a relief effort and bring food, water, oil and medicine to the disaster areas as quickly as possible.

The Japanese economy has sharply worsened. For example, stock prices have fallen below nine thousand and the yen has risen to 79 against the dollar.

If the government cannot correctly manage the Fukushima nuclear power plant accident, the Japanese economy will lose credibility from abroad.

Political circumstances have dramatically changed. Before the earthquake, Prime Minister Naoto Kan had been under the severe political pressure and the DPJ government was looking to be "knocked out" by the LDP and the KOMEITO in the near future.

However, after the earthquake, the atmosphere changed and the ruling and opposition parties need to cooperate to overcome such an unprecedented crisis. The political struggle entered armistice.

It will probably take a long time and a lot of money for the government to support the lives of people struck by the quake and rebuild infrastructure in these areas.

Therefore the next general election will be postponed indefinitely. Japan was unfortunately struck by a massive earthquake, but Prime Minister Naoto Kan was politically helped by the disaster, which might turn into a political trouble for Japan.

The Great East Japan Earthquake, Disaster area, Miyagi Prefecture.

Political Circumstances after the Earthquake
(April 2011)

Many people are beginning to doubt the quality of Prime Minister Naoto Kan. After the earthquake and tsunami, his leadership has often confused people, especially in terms of the Fukushima nuclear power plant accident.

According to the press coverage, it was reported that he has been irritated with the Fukushima situation, and exploded with anger to others around him. If this is true, I doubt his quality as a Prime Minister. The Prime Minister has the highest status and supreme power in Japan and he is required to overcome his weaknesses and stay calm and bold whatever the circumstances.

The Great East Japan Earthquake, Disaster area Kesennuma City, Miyagi Prefecture.

The fiscal 2011 first supplementary budget has been delayed and has not been submitted to the Diet. The decision making of the DPJ government is very slow compared to that of the LDP for the massive Hanshin Awaji earthquake years earlier. It seems that a lot of bureaucrats are surprised by the slow pace of the DPJ government and hesitate to propose new ideas since the government tends to dodge taking responsibility for their decisions.

The Ozawa faction protests that Prime Minister Naoto Kan should resign soon. The President of the LDP, Sadakazu Tanigaki believes that if Prime Minister Naoto Kan resigns, the LDP may become the ruling party. Moreover, on April 10, the DPJ was defeated in the unified local election, which resulted in a loss of power.

The Great East Japan Earthquake, Disaster area, Minami Sanriku Town, Miyagi Prefecture.

However, it is true that the opposition party has had difficulties in presenting censure motion against the Kan Cabinet since the Fukushima nuclear power plant accident. Therefore, for the meanwhile, the ruling and the opposition parties are forced to cooperate in the aftermath of the earthquake.

The Great East Japan Earthquake, Disaster area, Miyagi Prefecture.

When will Prime Minister Naoto Kan resign?
(June 2011)

On June 1, 2011, the LDP and the KOMEITO parties submitted a no-confidence motion against the Kan Cabinet to the Lower House. More than seventy members of the DPJ who chiefly belonged to the Ozawa faction, with complaints about Prime Minister Naoto Kan, showed their will to agree with the motion. If eighty-two members of the DPJ agree, the no-confidence motion will be passed, throwing the DPJ into confusion.

On June 2, before the vote, a meeting among the Lower House members of the DPJ was held, where Prime Minister Naoto Kan stated his resignation plan after the reconstruction from the disaster advances to a certain level.

Before the Lower House meeting of the DPJ, Mr. Hatoyama had negotiated with Mr. Kan and he had promised to resign in the near future.

For this reason, those seventy who had expressed agreement to the no-confidence motion changed their mind, and as a result, the motion was rejected.

However, on June 3, Mr. Kan insisted that he will continue as Prime Minister until the Fukushima nuclear power plant cooling system stabilizes, which means Mr. Kan had no intention to resign in the near future.

Mr. Hatoyama was surprised and angered to hear that and said he was easily taken in by Mr. Kan's performance. The Ozawa faction members also had expected Mr. Kan's resignation by June 30.

The reason for which the no-confidence motion was rejected was that most of the DPJ members wanted to avoid the dissolution of the House of Representatives.

Since the Great East Japan Earthquake on March 11, the LDP and the KOMEITO have cooperated with the Kan Cabinet as much as possible, but the action taken by the Kan Cabinet has been very slow and confusing to the people, especially in terms of the Fukushima nuclear power plant accident.

We doubted the quality of Mr. Kan as a Prime Minister. The opposition parties have to say what they think is right, and that is why we submitted a no-confidence motion against the Kan Cabinet to the Diet.

Circumstances in the aftermath of the Earthquake, from the fisheries cooperative, Kesennuma City.

Why has the DPJ Administration failed?
(August 2011)

It has only been a short two years since the DPJ administration began, but many people think that the DPJ administration has failed. Why can't the DPJ succeed? There are several factors.

Since most DPJ politicians are very young and short of experience, they have not been very successful in organizing the party. In fact, one young minister has repeatedly made crucial misjudgments in terms of some important matters.

Of course, the biggest reason for their failure is that both Mr. Hatoyama and Mr. KAN might lack the proficient qualities of Prime Minister. The DPJ consists of many factions but surprisingly, share no common philosophy throughout the party, called "KOURYO" in Japanese.

This philosophy is standard for decision making. The manifest is the target of their policy, but this is different from philosophy. For this reason, the DPJ have been in dispute with each other whenever they face difficult problems or accidents.

It takes about 16.8 trillion yen for the DPJ to realize their manifest. Before the change of government, the DPJ arrogantly promised that their manifest could be easily achieved by reducing wasteful spending and through the transformation of the national budget. However, the DPJ government couldn't secure the revenue for their manifest.

Moreover, the non-bureaucratic led government the DPJ promised ultimately resulted in failure. They excessively excluded bureaucrats to participate in the decision making of the government. As a result, bureaucrats resisted to cooperate with the DPJ government.

Thus the failure of DPJ administration.

A New Year's speech, Kyoto City, 2012.

Should Japan stop Nuclear Power Generation?

(December 2011)

It is true that the Fukushima nuclear power plant accident is serious, and many people think that Japan should stop producing nuclear power generation altogether. But the non nuclear power generation policy that Prime Minister Naoto Kan has stated has to be discussed from various viewpoints.

If all the nuclear power plants in Japan stopped, the power supply would fall short of about 30% of the power demand, which will urge industries to leave Japan.

The cause of the Fukushima No. 1 nuclear power plant accident must be sufficiently inspected. The Fukushima No. 2 nuclear power plant was also hit by the Great East Japan earthquake and tsunami, but it escaped serious damage because the height of the tsunami was 2 meters lower than that of the No. 1 plant and the emergency power remained active.

If the breakwater at the No.1 plant had been constructed a little higher, the accident might not have occurred.

I don't think that a non nuclear power generation policy is possible. Given instability of renewable energy, modern civilization wouldn't be realized for the time being without nuclear power generation.

If we strengthen counter-measures against massive earthquakes and tsunamis, the government can restart to the operations of the nuclear power plants that sit idle awaiting inspections.

Germany decided to seek a society that does not depend on nuclear power generation, but to purchase electricity from France where nuclear power generation continues. What do you think of the non nuclear power generation policy of Germany?

Inspection of the disaster area in Miyagi Prefecture.

From Two Party Politics to a Three Party Era
(December 2011)

Since single-seat constituency elections were first introduced in 1996, two party politics has steadily improved. Especially after the symbolic event of the DPJ that deprived the LDP of power in the Lower House general election of 2009.

However, most people think that the DPJ administration has failed. Mr. Noda took office as the third Prime Minister of the DPJ, but it seems to be difficult for him to overcome the weaknesses in his organization. Mr. Hachiro, who was once appointed Ministry of Economy, Trade and Industry, resigned only eight days later due to a slip of tongue.

I anticipate that the DPJ will be defeated in the next Lower House election. However, as long as single-seat constituency elections continue, two party politics will survive.

On the contrary, two major parties tend to conflict bitterly with each other. If the ruling party doesn't have a majority in both Houses of the Diet, the government will lack stability and political circumstance will be thrown into confusion.

As a result, a third party is required to bind together the two major parties. It is necessary for the third party to think what the right thing is for the nation and to persuade the two major parties to accept an appropriate compromise.

Therefore, the KOMEITO holds an extremely important position. It was the KOMEITO that actually proposed reforming child allowances and leading both the DPJ and LDP to accept the proposal.

The DPJ wants to persuade the KOMEITO over to their side. As does the LDP. The DPJ, LDP and the KOMEITO has agreed to reform major policies of the DPJ, such as child allowance and the free highway plan.

The era of three party politics has begun, leaving two party politics in it's wake.

My supporters rally, in Tokyo.

The Trans Pacific Partnership (TPP)

(January 2012)

Prime Minister Yoshihiko Noda decided to join the TPP negotiation on November 18, however, this doesn't mean that the Diet will agree on the TPP treaty.

There are many anti-TPP groups who protest that this will destroy agriculture, health insurance, and protected industries.

According to a theory of economics, it is true that the TPP will reduce regulation, increase supply, and accelerate deflation. However it is reported that the GDP will only grow by 0.56% over the next decade if Japan joins the TPP.

Moreover, the Government didn't fulfill its responsibility to explain the benefits and non benefits of the TPP, and it's a matter of course that the Government was strongly condemned for this action. Even the KOMEITO couldn't help but criticize the decision-making process of the government.

However, from my point of view, I don't necessarily oppose the TPP. Due to the yen's steep appreciation, production facilities can not help but move overseas, which has been termed the "hollowing out of industry". It is important for Japan to make a free trade accord with many countries.

In the near future, the TPP may urge China to open its market and remove barriers for trade and investment, which will lead to benefits for both China and the TPP groups. Actually, China insists on making a new economic group between the ASEAN plus 6 countries.

On the other hand, if the TPP intends to exclude China, China will become angry and may make a FTA with the EU. In this case, the amount of export to China from Japan will decrease substantially and Japan will be disadvantaged against the EU. Therefore, Japan should make every effort to expand free trade policies through the TPP.

The Tokyo Port.

The Beginning of the End for the DPJ Administration
(January 2012)

Prime Minister Yoshihiko Noda is eager to raise the consumption tax rate from 5% to 10% by 2015 due to the ever-growing budget deficit. The amount of public bonds will surpass ¥1,000 trillion in the near future.

However, the Ozawa group of the DPJ, which consists of about 100 Diet members, clearly oppose hiking the consumption tax rate. Instead, they insist that Japans' economy has been under deflation for a long time and that a raise of the rate will accelerate deflation.

If the DPJ government submits the consumption tax hike bill to the Diet in March, the Ozawa group may leave the DPJ and create a new party, which would mean more difficulties for the governments' management. As a result, the DPJ may lose the majority in the Lower House.

Nevertheless, the Diet deliberation of the bill will start. But as the DPJ can't pass the bill in both Houses of the Diet, if the bill is denied in the Lower House, then Prime Minister Noda will have to decide on the dissolution of the Lower House and hold a general election.

In the next Lower House general election, the DPJ will be defeated and the LDP will regain victory. At the same time, the KOMEITO, MINNA NO TO and ISHIN NO KAI, founded by Mayor of Osaka City Toru Hashimoto, may increase Diet members.

It is not easy to forecast which combination of new ruling parties will prevail, but I suppose that the DPJ may be divided and collapse.

The Reason the KOMEITO agreed to the Consumption Tax hike

(August 2012)

On June 15, 2012, the DPJ, LDP and the KOMEITO agreed to amend the consumption tax hike and social security reform bills. There are many people who oppose the consumption tax hike; however, social security costs surpassed 100 trillion yen in 2011 and the amount of issued public bonds is approaching 1,000 trillion yen.

Before the change of government in 2009, the ruling parties, the LDP and the KOMEITO had decided on tax system reform including a consumption tax hike to curtail increasing social security costs. However, the DPJ took control in the 2009 election, becoming the ruling party and insisted they could secure 16.8 trillion yen by cutting budget waste, and a consumption tax hike was unnecessary.

Nevertheless, the third Prime Minister of the DPJ, Yoshihiko Noda submitted a bill to increase the consumption tax to the Diet in 2012. It was only natural for the opposition parties to accuse the DPJ on the contradiction of policy and as a result, through a long Diet session, Noda admitted that the major DPJ policies presented in their manifest in 2009 could not be implemented.

I suppose the KOMEITO is responsible for a fiscal reconstruction and we can't disengage from the three party talks to amend the consumption tax hike bills. If we don't participate, public opinion will criticize the KOMEITO by saying they don't deserve to be a ruling party.

Therefore, it is better for us to reflect our policies to this amendment, such as changing the pension system, reduced consumption tax rate, and a child support system. It wouldn't be undesirable for the nation to allow the two biggest parties, the DPJ and LDP to decide the details of tax and social security reforms.

The KOMEITO required five conditions to support this legislation, and the DPJ swallowed them all. That is why the KOMEITO agreed upon the bills.

Elderly care facility, Yamaguchi Prefecture.

How can Japan overcome Deflation?
(August 2012)

I delivered a discussion on the Japanese economy during an intensive Diet deliberation for the budget committee on February 23 broadcasted on NHK, which resulted in a growing interest in the KOMEITO's economic policy.

I would like to introduce the summary of my session.

Japan has been suffering from deflation since 1996. There is no other advanced country except Japan which suffers from deflation. What is the reason behind the deflation in Japan? Generally, it is said that this is due to a huge shortage of demand. But I want to point out two factors.

First of all, developing countries like China and South Korea have exported a lot of industrial products to Japan over the last 20 years, and as a result, prices for goods such as televisions and personal computers have fallen to half the price they were of 20 years ago.

Second, a short term interest rate in Japan has been near zero since 1998, since Japan had to overcome a subsequent recession after the collapse of the bubble economy in 1991 and the Asian financial crisis in 1998. However, the Japanese economy could not easily recover.

For these reason, the Bank of Japan (BOJ) has continued the zero interest rate policy. Under this policy, the money easing policy of the BOJ is ineffective, since an increase of money supply can't lower interest rates any further. As a result, investment and consumption has not increased.

This economic situation is defined as "The Trap of Liquidity" by Professor J. M. Keynes. Short and long term interest rates in other advanced countries are higher than Japan. Under this economic circumstance, these measures need a fiscal policy, such as public works projects and eco-point system.

However, child allowance is the wrong policy as a measure against deflation, because people who receive it tend not to spend, but instead save.

Therefore the DPJ economic policy against deflation has not gone well.

Resuming stalled construction of the New Meishin Highway through Budget Committee deliberations to overcome deflation.

Can the LDP take back Power?
(August 2012)

It is well known that the DPJ, LDP and the KOMEITO all agreed to the consumption tax hike bill in order to ensure revenue for social security. The KOMEITO especially made this decision with consideration of the social security system and the fiscal reconstruction of Japan.

The consumption tax hike and social security reform bills were passed through after 129 hours of deliberation in the Lower House on July 26, 2012, then they were discussed for another 80 hours in the Upper House.

However, the LDP suddenly changed strategy and instead used the passage of these bills as political leverage, and wanted to submit a no confidence motion or censure motion before voting on the bills. The LDP was eager to exchange the dissolution of the Lower House for the passage of these bills, which meant virtually abandoning the three party agreement.

This tactic shows that the LDP lacks responsibility to the nation and only moves in accordance with their own political circumstances. The KOMEITO was embarrassed and nearly lost confidence with the LDP at the time.

Such political tactics used by the LDP can't be understood by the people and even if the LDP wins in the next general election, managing the LDP administration will be difficult and unstable.

I suppose that the LDP management is similar to that of the DPJ. Many people hope that the ruling party has a clear philosophy and is strongly united, but the future of Japanese politics looks desperate.

Speech, the anniversary of the end of the war, August 15, 2012.

Chapter II

The Liberal Democratic Party / The KOMEITO Ruling Coalition

"Abenomics" dramatically changed the economic condition of Japan. Owing to Abenomics, the Japanese economy has been overcoming deflation. On the other hand, the 2014 consumption tax hike has resulted in a decline of "real wages", leading to a curb in consumption. To overcome deflation depends on a further raise of pay levels.

As for foreign affairs, there was a pile of crucial and controversial agendas such as "Security Legislations" in terms of the right to Collective Self-Defense and past conflicts between Japan and China.

Nevertheless, the Abe administration has overcome these difficulties, and as a result, Mr. Abe will be the longest serving Prime Minister of Japan from November 2019. Why can the Abe administration retain power for such a long time?

To answer this question, we can't forget the important role of the KOMEITO that has supported the LDP on policies and elections. The stability of the LDP and KOMEITO ruling coalition has led to long term economic growth, expansion of social welfare, education, and so forth.

New Year's party at the Kyoto Prefectural Headquarter of the KOMEITO.

My supporters rally, Ide Town, Kyoto Prefecture, 2013.

The Start of the Second LDP and KOMEITO Ruling Coalition
(January 2013)

On December 16, 2012, the DPJ was defeated in the general election as I had forecasted, with the LDP winning a landslide victory and the KOMEITO, increasing 10 seats from 21 to 31.

Before the election, several new parties were suddenly established, such as the Japan Restoration Party led by former Tokyo Governor Shintaro Ishihara and Osaka Mayor Toru Hashimoto, and the Tomorrow Party headed by Yukiko Kada and Ichiro Ozawa.

However, this new "Third Force" could not expand as largely as expected. The reason being that these new parties could not show a clear political philosophy since their leaders had conflicting ideas with each other but forcibly united anyway for victory in the election.

The new coalition government has faced many problems and concerns, such as deflation of the economy, the Senkaku Islands issue with China, nuclear power generation, the TPP, and so on.

The most urgent of these problems is the reconstruction of the Japanese economy. Especially, regional economies and small-medium companies are still facing severe economic conditions.

The new government has already urged the BOJ to ease money supplies and will increase public works projects to defend peoples' livelihoods from disaster, which will in turn, expand domestic demands and lead to recovery from deflation.

I was elected for a third term in this election and my first appointment as a Parliamentary Secretary for the Financial Minister for the Abe Cabinet. I will use this position for the development of peoples' livelihoods.

Parliamentary Secretaries of the Abe Cabinet. Yuzuru TAKEUCHI, front row, first from the right, 2012.

What is "Abenomics"?

(March 2013)

After a change in government and the introduction of Abenomics, a term coined for the economic policies of the Abe administration, the yen has dropped back to the level of ¥93 against the dollar from ¥79, and the Nikkei average has risen from the level of ¥8,000 to ¥12,000.

Abenomics consists of three points; the first is a bold monetary easing policy by the BOJ, second is a fiscal policy for public works projects, and third is a strategy of economic growth including deregulation of medical care and agriculture. These policies have been branded "The Three Arrows".

Prime Minister Shinzo Abe especially urged the BOJ to increase the monetary base much further than the previous administration setting up a "2% inflation target policy", which has been surprisingly effective to the stock and foreign exchange markets.

Inflation target policies have already been adopted by the Federal Reserve Bank (FRB) in the U.S. and several central banks in other countries. However, it is the first time for the BOJ to implement such a policy.

This social and economic experiment undertaken by the government has resulted in success, and the atmosphere of society has undoubtedly been improving. Exporting companies have rapidly increased profits by the yen's depreciation and stock price appreciation. As a result, capital investment will soon follow.

The most important point is whether enterprises can raise pay levels for employees. Mr. Abe knows this well and recently requested the Federation of Economic Organization to increase pay levels.

Without raising pay levels, the 2% inflation policy would make laborers suffer. However, if several companies actually begin to raise pay levels, then this trend will spread gradually, leading to an increase in consumption.

Thus, I am convinced that this monetary easing policy originating from Milton Freedman, a fiscal policy originating from John Maynard Keynes and an innovation policy originating from Joseph A Schumpeter, are indispensable for Japan to overcome deflation.

Large rally at the Kyoto Prefectural Headquarter of the KOMEITO.

The Political Relevance of the 2013 Upper House Election

(August 2013)

In the Upper House election held on July 21, 2013, the LDP and its coalition, the KOMEITO, won a landslide victory taking a combined 76 of the 121 seats in the 242-member chamber. As a result, the ruling coalition parties secured a majority both in the Lower and the Upper Houses. Recently, Japanese politics has suffered from a twisted Diet making many people desire political stability, which led to the LDP and the KOMEITO win.

Political stability has resulted in a positive effect to Japanese economy and Prime Minister Shinzo Abe has vowed to overcome long time deflation of the economy through "Abenomics".

Furthermore, Mr. Abe is eager to revise the Constitution, especially article 9, which includes a change of interpretation by the Government to give the Self Defense Force a larger military role.

However, Natsuo Yamaguchi, the KOMEITO leader, clearly opposes the interpretation change of article 9. The LDP has a majority in the Lower House but not in the Upper House. Therefore the importance of the KOMEITO will become larger.

There are many difficult agendas that the Abe administration has to face, such as raising the consumption tax rate from 5% to 8%, the TPP, and reconstruction efforts from the Great East Japan earthquake. It will be better for Mr. Abe to set aside his nationalistic agenda.

For other election results, the DPJ was crushed and the Japan Restoration Party couldn't expand their seats due to its co-leader Mr. Hashimoto's gaffes on Japan's wartime "comfort women" system. On the other hand, the Japan Communist Party expanded to some extent due to low voter turnouts, which often work in favor for an organized party, and because "Abenomics" might not be beneficial to some people.

To conclude, no one knows what may happen tomorrow in politics. The ruling bloc politicians should be prudent in administration management and mind their gaffes.

The Ministry of Finance, France.
Discussion on the reduced consumption tax rate system, 2013.

Consumption tax hike and reduced tax rate
(January 2014)

The most important issue facing the Japanese economy is to achieve both recovery from deflation and fiscal reconstruction.

Prime Minister Shinzo Abe has prudently discussed that recovery from deflation is possible in spite of a rise in the consumption tax rate. The annual GDP ratio from April to June was 3.8% and other economic indicators and indexes have performed well. On October 1, 2013, Mr. Abe decided to raise the consumption tax rate from 5% to 8% starting April 2014.

The purpose of the consumption tax hike is to secure financial resources for the increasing costs in social security, which leads to a lower issuance of national bonds that currently stand at 700 trillion

The Bank of England, London, 2013. Yuzuru TAKEUCHI, third from the right.

European School of Management and Technology (ESMT), Berlin, 2013.

yen.

On the other hand, after the consumption tax hike, it is thought that consumption and investment will fall flat for a while. Therefore, in order to overcome deflation, the government has established an economic package consisting of 1 trillion yen for tax reduction, and 5 trillion yen for the supplementary budget.

Most domestic and foreign economists appreciate this decision; however, a few in the media doubt that if the government spends 5 trillion yen on a supplementary budget, a 3% hike will be ineffective for fiscal consolidation.

However, funds for this economic package are not from the consumption tax hike, but instead, from the surplus remaining from 2012 account settlement and the increase from 2013's original tax revenue.

Forthcoming challenges Japan faces are whether raising the consumption tax rate from 8% to 10% in October 2015 and introducing reduced tax rate for foods, newspaper etc., are possible.

The KOMEITO insists on the introduction of a consumption tax rate reduction system for low incomers when the standard rate reach-

Mr. Bernard CAZENEUVE, Minister of Finance, France, 2013.

The Bank of France, Paris, 2013.

es 10%. This is a controversial issue between the LDP and the KOMEITO, but on December 12 after overnight deliberations, both parties agreed to introduce this system on condition securing the financial resources and an understanding from tax payment companies.

The economic management of the Japanese government is being watched around the world.

Taj Mahal, India, 2014.

A visit to India
(February 2014)

Mr. Yamaguchi, the KOMEITO leader and member of the House of Councilors, Mr. Okamoto and myself, vice directors of the international office of the KOMEITO and members of the House of Representatives were invited to India by the Indian government from January 5 to 12, 2014.

His and Her Imperial Majesty visited India last November for the first time in 50 years and subsequently, Prime Minister Abe participated in the Republic Day ceremony of India as the chief guest on January 26. It is obvious that the Indian government has been putting an emphasis on the Japan-India relationship.

While in India, we had a conference with Prime Minister Manmohan Shin and other VIPs, and agreed to strengthen cooperation in terms of economy and education for both countries. Mr. Shin emphasized that he understands the political role and achievements of the KOMEITO over the past 50 years since its establishment. And he said that the grass root network, consisting of about 3,000 local assembly members is wonderful.

The Indian economy has developed tremendously and its GDP average rate during the past 10 years was 8.6%, while the inflation rate is at the same level as the GDP rate. About 30 years ago, SUZUKI motors, the Japanese automobile manufacturer, built factories and started to supply vehicles in Delhi, and as a result, there are many traffic jams occurring everywhere in Indian cities.

The IT industries are strong in India but other manufacturing industries are still weak prompting the Indian government's desire to develop Japanese enterprises, particularly in electronics to encourage investment in India.

In Delhi, the Japanese government (JICA) financed about 60% of the construction for the underground railway that currently consists of 190 km, and will expand to 300 km by 2017.

A caste system still remains in India, however, Indian society is based on liberalism and democracy, and therefore, if a person succeeds in business, or receives a good education, that person will not face discrimination. I suppose that India will continue to grow just as China did over the next 15 years with the assistance of Japan. Therefore, Japan will need to rethink its foreign affairs from a new point of view.

Mr. Salman Khurshid, Foreign Minister of India, Dehli, 2014. Yuzuru TAKEUCHI, first from the left. Natsuo YAMAGUCHI, Chief Representative of the KOMEITO, second from the right.

Can a Cabinet reinterpret Article 9 of the Constitution?

(March 2014)

Article 9 of Japan's Constitution is famous for the "Renunciation of War". This interpretation of article 9 states that Japan has the right to self-defense, but is not allowed to exercise the right of collective self-defense which is authorized in international laws. The Japanese government has maintained this interpretation for over 60 years since the enforcement of the Constitution; however, Prime Minister Abe is eager for his Cabinet to reinterpret article 9 giving Japan the ability to exercise the right of collective self-defense.

Mr. Abe and his group think that the security situation in the East Asia region has changed and has become strained due to threats by China and North Korea, prompting Japan to strengthen the Japan-U.S. alliance through the reinterpretation of article 9. However, the Cabinet Legislation Bureau is prudent in the reinterpretation of article 9. Mr. Yamaguchi, the KOMEITO leader, has warned that the government should politely explain the reason for this reinterpretation and consider it's impact on the international community, in particular, on East Asian nations.

Article 9 was realized based on deep reflection of World War II and has been supported as a "fortress for peace" for over 60 years by most of the Japanese population. If the Abe Cabinet allows for the exercise of collective self-defense, Japan will be obligated to go to war for the allied nations despite no direct attack on Japan from a third country. This will change the direction and the shape of Japan considerably as a peaceful nation. This point is extremely important; however, it may go unnoticed by most of the Japanese people.

The schedule Mr. Abe wants is as follows: In April, the Prime Minister's private panel will propose a security report to Mr. Abe. Subsequently, a discussion regarding this issue will start between the LDP and the KOMEITO, and if an agreement by both parties is reached, Mr. Abe will try to secure Cabinet approval for the reinterpretation of Article 9 by the end of summer. Afterwards, the Cabinet decision will be deliberated in the Diet, since revisions of related laws will be needed for the Self-Defense Forces to act according to the new interpretation.

The Cabinet Meeting of the Abe administration, Prime Minister's Office. Yuzuru TAKEUCHI, second from the left.

Nevertheless, there are a few opponents, not only in the KOMEITO, but also in the LDP. It is indispensable for Mr. Abe to have sufficient discussion with the ruling parties and to propose the disputed points to the Japanese people through Diet deliberations paying careful attention to public opinion.

Reply to the opposition, the House of Councilors. Yuzuru TAKEUCHI, center.

Should Japan reduce the corporate tax rate?
(May 2014)

As you know, "Abenomics" consists of 3 points; the first is a bold monetary easing policy, the second is a flexible fiscal policy and the third is a strategy for economic growth, such as deregulation and so on. To date, the first and the second policies have yielded good outcomes; therefore, whether Abenomics can succeed will depend on its third policy, a strategy for economic growth.

On the other hand, the Abe Cabinet has implemented a consumption tax hike from 5% to 8% last April in order to reduce the issuance of public bonds that stands at 7 trillion yen, and to secure social security financial resources.

To decrease the burden of the consumption tax hike, the Abe Cabinet and our coalition party have urged the Japan Business Federation to raise employee wages, which has resulted in many enterprises beginning to do so.

Hereafter, the most controversial policy will be to reduce the corporate tax. Prime Minister Shinzo Abe is eager to lower the corporate tax rate as a growth strategy that will lead to expanding fiscal deficit, without taking any other measures.

In Japan, the substantial rate of corporate tax, including local tax is about 35%, which is relatively higher than most emerging and developed countries.

I heard that in Germany the substantial corporate tax rate is about

29%. If Japan lowers corporate tax rate to the level of Germany, we should prepare alternative financial resources of 3 trillion yen. We have to verify whether lower corporate tax rates really strengthen enterprises and encourage economic growth.

Board Meeting of the MOF. Yuzuru TAKEUCHI, center row, second from the right.

Cabinet decision on the right of Collective Self-Defense to ensure Japan's survival and protect its people
(August 2014)

On July 1, 2014, Abe Cabinet has made a decision on the right of collective self-defense to ensure Japan's survival and protect its people. To date, under article 9 of Japan's Constitution, Japan has the right of self-defense, but is not allowed to exercise the right of collective self-defense. Has Japan reinterpreted article 9 of the Constitution? The answer is No.

Article 9 of the Constitution prohibits Japan from exercising the so-called "right of collective self-defense" for defending other countries. However, this Cabinet decision on the right of collective self-defense is to ensure Japan's survival and protect its people.

The security environment surrounding Japan has been fundamentally transformed by shifts in the global power balance, the rapid progress of technological innovation, and threats such as weapons of mass destruction, and so on. Even an armed attack occurring against a foreign country could actually threaten Japan's survival.

When an armed attack against the U.S. occurs and as a result, threatens Japan's survival and poses a clear danger to fundamentally overturn people's right to life, liberty and pursuit of happiness, and when there is no other appropriate means available to repel the attack and ensure Japan's survival and protect its people, use of force to the minimum extent necessary should be permitted under the Constitution as measures for self-defense. This is the conclusion of the Cabinet decision within the limit of the basic logic of the interpretation of Article 9 of the Constitution, which is permitted under the Constitution for defending Japan.

This Cabinet decision is based on the agreement that has been bitterly discussed between the LDP and the KOMEITO from on May 15 to July 1. In the KOMEITO, the possibility of leaving the coalition government was debated, however, they reached the conclusion that if other opposition parties, such as "Jisedai no To" (The Party For Future Generations) and "Minna no To" (Your Party) admit full-scale use for the right of collective self-defense under the Abe administration, Japan will be really dragged into wars in the near future, which would be a very regrettable circumstances.

State Ministers Meeting of the Abe Cabinet. Yuzuru TAKEUCHI, center row, first from the left, Prime Minister's Office.

The LDP and KOMEITO retain a ruling coalition
(January 2015)

In the latest general election of the House of Representatives December 2014, the LDP and KOMEITO secured 326 seats (LDP 291; KOMEITO 35), which clinched over two-thirds for the 465-member Lower House, and maintained the ruling coalition. I was also able to secure my forth election win owing to the sincere support of party members and our supporters.

Last September, I was appointed to the first vice chairperson on Diet Policy Committee of the KOMEITO and the director of the House Steering Committee. I will strive to do my best in terms of

Diet Policy Committee between the ruling bloc and the opposition parties. Yuzuru TAKEUCHI, first from the right.

meaningful and comprehensive tasks in the management of Diet affairs, including plenary sessions.

Furthermore, as a member of the tax consultation meeting of the ruling coalition, we have decided to introduce a reduced rate of consumption tax for food products in 2017 in addition to lowering the corporate tax rate to enhance competitiveness of Japanese enterprises in the 2015 Outline of the Tax Revision of the LDP and KOMEITO.

Forthcoming, we will construct a strong network for the Japanese economy to include small and medium-sized enterprises and households to experience the Abenomics effect.

On November 17, 2014, the KOMEITO celebrated it's 50th anniversary. The principle of the KOMEITO is : hear the people, fight for the people, stand with the people. Based on this principle, we intend to win the unified local assembly elections in April.

Security Legislations are Constitutional

(September 2015)

On July 16, 2015, security legislations were passed in the House of Representatives and were sent to the House of Councilors for approval. The deliberations started on July 27 however, according to media outlets, it seems that many people feel the government's explanation of this legislation is insufficient.

Subsequently, the approval rating for the Abe Cabinet has declined for the first time since taking office. Many people don't understand why security legislations are needed and whether they are constitutional or not, and have concerns that Japan might get involved in other countries' wars in the future.

The Abe Cabinet and the ruling party, the LDP and KOMEITO, have planned security legislation through detailed reviews over the last year. Therefore, we are convinced of the necessity and constitutionality of the legislations and have confidence that Japan will be able to deter wars using these security legislations.

In the House of Councilors the ruling coalition has a majority of seats, and in the House of Representatives they have two-thirds, therefore, there is a strong probability that security legislations will be enacted in this Diet.

However, the opposition parties and some media outlets have appealed the security legislations as unconstitutional, and have conducted bitter campaigns to discard these legislations. A specific op-

Chapter II The Liberal Democratic Party / The KOMEITO Ruling Coalition

position party seems to be creating revolutionary actions instead of arguing policy.

The purpose of the security legislations is to strengthen Japan's defense capability in accordance with the changes to the security environment surrounding Japan, and to contribute the peace and security for international society.

The security legislations admit the right of collective self-defense for the first time. However, its contents are extremely close to the right of individual self-defense to defend Japan, succeeding the basic logic of article 9 of the Constitution.

To date, the Cabinet Legislation Bureau has interpreted article 9 to prohibit Japan from exercising the so-called "Right of collective self-defense", which means that Japan can't use force to aid a foreign countries defense.

Therefore, security legislations permit Japan to use force to the minimum extent necessary when an armed attack against U.S. forces being dispatched for Japan's defense occurs and as a result threatens Japan's survival and poses a clear danger to fundamentally overturn people's right to life, liberty and pursuit of happiness, and when there is no other appropriate means available to repel the attack and ensure Japan's survival and protect its people.

It's a matter of course that the SDF is not permitted to be dispatched abroad under nonaggressive national security policies.

We would like to make a further effort to foster the people's comprehension of these security legislations.

My hopes as the State Minister of Health, Labor and Welfare

(December 2015)

I was appointed as the State Minister of Health, Labor and Welfare on October 9, 2015. The Ministry of Health, Labor and Welfare is an important and large authority that regulates a wide range of administrative fields that directly relates to the lives of people in the fields of medicine, welfare, nursing care, labor and pension.

Recently, Japan has been battling deflation through Abenomics, and Prime Minister Abe announced "Three New Arrows"; First is a strong economy policy, increasing the GDP for 2020 to the level of ¥600 trillion. Second is a child care support policy, aiming to raise the birth rate by 2020 to the level of 1.8. Third is a firm social secu-

The Center for iPS Cell Research and Application, Kyoto University. Prof. Shinya Yamanaka (left), Yuzuru TAKEUCHI (center), 2016.

rity policy, to create a society in which people need not leave their jobs due to concerns of family nursing care.

The growth of an economy does not necessarily lead to the happiness of an individual, rather, sustainable social security may be able to bring a positive effect to the macro-economy.

Through these "Three New Arrows", Prime Minister Abe shows his will to realize a "Society in which All Citizens are Dynamically Engaged". These contents are what the ruling coalition KOMEITO has always insisted upon. We aim to give relief and hope to people suffering from various obstacles such as income disparities, diseases and handicaps.

I am convinced that the Abe administration is on the right path to pursue an idealistic society.

Prof. Shinya Yamanaka, Nobel Laureate in Physiology or Medicine in 2012 for his work in iPS cells.

Right wing and Centrist Line VS. Left wing and Communist Line
(September 2016)

There were many controversial issues for the 2016 House of Councilors Election. Has Abenomics, an economic policy package, resulted in success or failure? Social security policies such as child and nursing care were undoubtedly disputed issues. The opposition parties were eager to focus on the revision of the Constitution, but the ruling coalition, the LDP and KOMEITO, avoided this issue since Diet deliberations were still immature.

However, I suppose the biggest issue of the election was whether people would choose a center - right agenda line of the LDP and KOMEITO, or a leftist agenda line of the Democratic Party (DP)

Discussions became complicated in the Budget Committee. Yuzuru TAKEUCHI, center of a dispute.

and Japan Communist Party (JCP).

The DP was formed by a merger of the DPJ and Ishin in 2016, of which members were mostly liberal and a few conservative, not least, communist.

However, the DP amazingly collaborated with the JCP and they ran unified candidates in 32 prefectural constituencies against the ruling bloc in order to abolish the peace and security laws, enacted last year, and to convert Abenomics to any other economic policy.

The DP states that the Self Defense Force and the Japan-US alliance are constitutional, on the other hand, JCP views both as unconstitutional. How do they defend Japan after abolishing the peace and security laws? I can't understand their vision regarding security.

Neither opposition parties have presented a concrete economic policy to overcome deflation. In this election, the alliance of these

New Year speech, Kyoto City, 2017.

opposition parties resulted in failure because of inadequate presentation in terms of these issues to the people, and as a result, allowed the ruling bloc to win two-thirds of the seats in the Upper House.

Nevertheless, the DP and JCP plan to cooperate in the upcoming House of Representatives election. The JCP is the party to realize the revolution of communism, and in fact, had implemented many violent activities in the 1950's. However, nowadays many people don't know this history. Does the DP?

Budget Committee, the House of Representatives.

An Era of Division and Conflict
(January 2017)

On August, 2016, I resigned as the State Minister of Health, Labor and Welfare due to a Cabinet reshuffle, and was subsequently appointed as the Chairperson for the Committee on Internal Affairs and Communication in September.

Incidentally, in the U.S., Mr. Donald Trump won the presidential election on November 8 contrary to many intellectuals expectations, and similarly, the U.K. voted to leave the EU with heated arguments in their national referendum.

I call these phenomena "Rebellion by the Masses", which has

Visiting Estonia to inspect the circumstances of its digital government, 2017.

swept over advanced countries. We analyze that this division and conflict amongst people has deepened in accordance with globalization, and consequently, those who were left behind became poorer with their anger and complaints boiling over.

In Japan, if the middle class falls to a relative poverty class, our society will come to risk as the people will start saying what they really think, bearing their disappointment.

Therefore, the KOMEITO has confirmed these two points; first, it is important to maintain the LDP-KOMEITO ruling coalition and stabilize the political system. Political stability will bring economic growth, which leads to increases in tax revenue and the expansion of social security and education.

Second, the KOMEITO from now on has to implement various

Mr. Sven Sester, Chairman, Economic Affairs Committee, Parliament of Estonia.

kinds of policies by standing closer with the people, hearing people's voices and researching their potential needs.

The U.S. President Donald Trump pledged to put "America First", and to strengthen the priority of national interests through trade and foreign exchange intervention. However, his speech appears to promote division and conflict on foreign relations.

We forecast a tough negotiation between the U.S. and Japan, but fundamentally, it is necessary for Japan to enhance economic and social security policies in order to protect the livelihoods of low income people while increasing the middle class, which will lead to better unity in Japan.

Inspection in the aftermath of the 2016 Kumamoto Earthquake. Yuzuru TAKEUCI, Chairperson for the Committee on Internal Affairs and Communication, center.

A Turning Point for the Abe Administration
(July 2017)

The LDP was unprecedentedly defeated in the Tokyo Metropolitan Assembly Election on July 2, winning only 23 seats, their worst result, and less than half of their pre-vote presence. Governor Yuriko Koike's party "Tomin First no Kai" and its allies including the KOMEITO won a landslide victory, taking 79 seats of the 127-member Tokyo Metropolitan Assembly.

I suppose that the most important reason for the LDP's defeat was the failure of the Abe administration itself, such as the shadow of suspicions over cronyism for his friend's school "Kakei Gakuen", gaffes by the SDF Minister Inada Tomomi, a Diet member Toyoda Mayuko's violence against her secretary, and so on.

Just before voting day, Prime Minister Abe gave a speech on a street corner to support a candidate for the Tokyo Metropolitan Assembly, and there happened to be a demonstration asking for his resignation. Upon hearing the protest, Mr. Abe suddenly said that he will never fail to surrender to such people, however, this incurred public censure of the Abe Cabinet. As a result, its approval rate fell sharply from 50% to 30%.

The KOMEITO, the ruling coalition on the national level, decided to cooperate with "Tomin First no Kai" in the Tokyo Metropolitan Assembly Election, and was able to maintain their 23 seats, the same as their pre-vote presence. This was another reason for the LDP's defeat.

On the other hand, the opposition Democratic Party decreased 10 seats from 15 to 5, while the Japan Communist Party increased only 2 seats from 17 to 19. Most people in Tokyo didn't have the desire to convert to the DP and the JCP regime.

Nevertheless, it won't be easy for Mr. Abe to recover from his approval rate. He is eager to realize the revision of the Constitution, especially Article 9, by 2020. However, if his low approval rate continues, the Constitutional Amendment will be difficult.

What most people want is a raise in their wages by overcoming deflation and an economic recovery, and to have the hope in their livelihoods by further developing social security and child care.

Fuji TV program, Discussions on the shadow of suspicions over cronyism for Mr. Abe's friends school "Kakei Gakuen".

The House
of Representatives General Election 2017
(November 2017)

Early morning on September 17, I awoke to see an NHK news report that stated Prime Minister Shinzo Abe would dissolve the House of Representatives at the beginning of the Extraordinary Diet on September 28. Even I, a member of the ruling bloc, was very surprised and hurried to confirm the credibility of the news.

There were several reasons for this snap election. The first was that North Korea's nuclear weapons and ballistic missiles were becoming a serious threat to Japan, and Abe needed to create a strong regime. The second was that Abe and the KOMEITO agreed to reduce the

Campaign speech, Kyoto City, 2017.

educational burden of parents by widening the use of the consumption tax which was initially for the purpose of social security.

After the dissolution, Tokyo Metropolitan Governor, Yuriko Koike became the head of "Kibo no To" which was founded to compete in national politics. At that time many people highly expected that "Kibo no To" might grow to be a major party and win the general election as she did for the Tokyo metropolitan assembly election in July. Therefore, Seiji Maehara, head of the DP, decided that the DP would unite with "Kibo no To" at the general meeting of the DP Diet members.

However, Koike expressed her intention to eliminate the DP Diet members who didn't agree with her policies, especially for the peace and security bills that the DP had thoroughly opposed in 2015, and therefore, Mr. Edano, a left wing DP Lower House member, decided

Budget Committee, HR, December 2017.

to found a new party, the Constitutional Democratic Party of Japan(CDPJ). As a result, the DP members of the Lower House divided into three groups, Kibo no To, the CDPJ, and independents. Moreover, the support rate of Kibo no To also plummeted due to Koike's words, "get rid of".

Finally, the October 22 general election resulted in victory for the LDP-KOMEITO bloc, which obtained 313 seats, a two-thirds majority for the 465-member Lower House. The main reason for the victory was that many voters disliked the opposition parties' division and confusion, and voted for political stability.

On the other hand, there were many people, even amongst the LDP supporters, who didn't like the shadow of suspicion over cronyism for schools of Abe's friends, Moritomo and Kakei Gakuen. There were also concerns about Abe's militant character, which led to the CDPJ's advance as the main opposition party.

Prime Minister Shinzo Abe and the Cabinet members have to face people sincerely and humbly.

The Mission of the KOMEITO in the Abe Administration
(June 2018)

Prime Minister Shinzo Abe has been repeatedly pursued over the suspicion of cronyism for his friend's schools, Moritomo and Kakei Gakuen, from the opposition parties in the Diet session over this year.

I am the director of the Budget Committee for the House of Representatives. The opposition parties have seldom deliberated on serious foreign affairs such as denuclearization, missiles and the North Korean abduction issue, or on economic and fiscal agendas such as overcoming deflation and fiscal consolidation. Instead, they have focused on only Moritomo and Kakei Gakuen issues. That's abnormal.

The KOMEITO, a partner of the ruling coalition, is based on the principle of fairness, and agreed to summon Mr. Sagawa who was the former director general of the National Tax Administration Agency, as a sworn witness, and Mr. Yanase who had been a secretary for Prime Minister Abe, as an unsworn witness in the Budget Committee. As a representative of the KOMEITO, I questioned both of them.

However, in the Diet, there is a rule for summoning sworn witness, that it is limited to cases of suspicion over a penal offenses. Otherwise, it is easy for a political power to violate human rights by summoning a citizen to the Diet.

From this writing, Kakei Gakuen has not been recognized as illegal by criminal law in spite of the suspicion over cronyism on the administrative process.

Recently, the approval rate for Abe administration has been rising, while the supporting rates for the opposition parties have been lowering. Perhaps many people think that cronyism is not good, but they desire to discuss more important agendas such as North Korea, the economy and social security in the Diet.

The KOMEITO is a conservative and liberal party that has 54 Diet members (29 in the House of Representatives, 25 in the House of Councilors), and around 3,000 local assembly members. In the 2017 general election, the KOMEITO obtained about 7 million votes for proportional representation, which means that there were 25 thousand supporters in a single seat constituency on average.

The Prime Minister's Office.

Therefore, the KOMEITO is indispensable for the LDP to win in election.

The mission of the KOMEITO in the Abe administration is to steer the LDP by handling, braking, and accelerating, which leads to political stability and recovering the trust of the people.

Prime Minister Shinzo Abe, the official residence of Prime Minister.

How to stabilize a deteriorating global political environment
(February 2019)

In 2019, world political circumstances may affect Japanese politics. For example, conflicts between the U.S. and China in terms of technology and trade might further escalate, while the UK has caused tremendous confusion surrounding "Brexit". Furthermore, in France, President Macron has been facing mass demonstrations and riots, requiring redress of the tax disparity and the resignation of the president.

Given these circumstances, I suppose there are three takeaway points for Japan. The first is that political leaders have to act with wider perspectives, and not make political decisions on partial points of view. The second is that the government has to grapple with livelihoods and the sentiments of the masses. However, this doesn't mean the government gives into so-called "Populism". The third is that policy makers have to solve problems using common sense. In this world, there are many conflicts and controversial issues, but politicians need to be understanding to anyone with conflicting thoughts and provide sound ideas and resolve these issues with common sense. These three points are also important for the KOMEITO to follow through with.

In April, the unified local assembly elections will be held. On May 1st, the new Emperor will ascend the throne, and perhaps, the election of the House of Councilors will be held in July.

Chapter II The Liberal Democratic Party / The KOMEITO Ruling Coalition

In 2007, twelve years ago, the now defunct DPJ gained a solid victory for the unified local assembly elections, which gave impetus to the remarkable advance of the DPJ in the House of Councilors' election.

That is why the LDP-KOMEITO ruling coalition has already started to strengthen electoral cooperation between both parties.

The KOMEITO especially puts an emphasis on economic policies relating to the consumption tax hike which is scheduled to take effect on October 1. For example, we sought a reduced consumption tax rate for food, free education for children(0-5 age) and additional benefits for lower pension individuals.

It is crucial for the ruling bloc to prevent the middle class from dividing into a disparity between the wealthy and poor in our society.

Prof. Jörg Rocholl, the president of ESMT in Berlin, visited my Diet office, Tokyo, 2018.
ESMT=European School of Management and Technology

Can Human Race control Global Warming?
(March 2019)

Many scientists around the world insist that global warming has been accelerating due to the extensive use of fossil fuels and an increase in greenhouse gasses over several centuries, since the Industrial Revolution. This has led to abnormal climate changes such as unprecedented typhoons, extreme deluges, and deadly heat waves all over the world.

In order to reduce greenhouse gasses, the Kyoto Protocol was adopted among developed nations in 1997. However, developing nations such as China and India were not part in this protocol at first. The U.S., which emits the world's second largest volume of greenhouse gasses after China, withdrew from the protocol in 2001 stating it would restrain economic growth.

In 2015, the Paris Agreement, a new multilateral framework on climate change, was finally adopted among 190 nations including the U.S. and developing countries. It aims to combat the rise in average temperatures and to restrain temperatures by 2 degrees, comparative to the Industrial Revolution.

As a result, each nation was obligated to create their target plans, referred to as the "Nationally Determined Contribution", and to take domestic measures to reduce greenhouse gas emission. Nevertheless, the U.S. president, Donald Trump surprisingly withdrew from the agreement in 2017 since he believes global warming was "merely a hoax".

In accordance with the "Nationally Determined Contribution", each nation is required to implement concrete measures such as forest preservation, an introduction of carbon tax or emission trading, renewable energies, low emission vehicles, and other approaches for the reduction of greenhouse gasses and fossil fuels.

Of course, nuclear power generation might be thought as one of the measures for reducing greenhouse gasses, but in Japan, many people still fear the risk of radioactive contamination by nuclear power plant accidents such as what happened in the aftermath of the Great East Japan Earthquake.

Renewable energy sources are safe and clean technologies, but have several demerits such as high initial costs, unstable or insufficient power supplies which can lead to a negative impact on the

Disaster area, Kurama, Kyoto City, 2018.

economy.

Moreover, even if the "Nationally Determined Contribution" is impeccably implemented, it will be rather difficult to curb global warning. Humans must rally wisdoms to achieve any breakthroughs in global warming.

Disaster area, Ukyo ward, Kyoto City, 2012.

The Importance of the KOMEITO as a Centrist Party
(April 2019)

In Western Europe, so-called "Populist Parties" which include the far right and left, have rapidly gained in popularity due to the surging wave of anti-immigrant, anti-EU, and anti-globalism (protectionism) sentiment, while the centrist parties have been dwindling. This phenomenon seems to result in serious divisions and conflicts for each nation.

In Japan, on the other hand, political circumstances have been relatively stable since the Abe administration led by the LDP-KOMEITO ruling coalition started on December, 2012. The LDP is a conservative party and the KOMEITO is a centrist one.

The most important reason for political stability is that the KOMEITO has supported the LDP for both elections and policies. The KOMEITO, the fourth party in the Diet, holds 54 Diet members (29 in the House of Representatives, 35 in the House of Councilors), and was supported by around 7 million voters with a 6% approval rate for proportional representation in the 2017 Lower House election.

The fundamental principle of the KOMEITO is humanism that highly respects lives and livelihoods without depending on a specific ideology like Communism. The KOMEITO members always listen to various voices of the public and make efforts to reflect them in the government policies.

In contrast, opposition parties, such as the Constitutional Democratic Party of Japan (CDPJ), a left wing party, and the National Democratic Party (NDP), a center left party, are products of schism from the now defunct Democratic Party of Japan (DPJ). The DPJ had been the ruling party from September 2009 to December 2012.

Now the ruling bloc, the Liberal Democratic Party (LDP) accounts for the majority in both Houses (283 seats for the 465-member House of Representatives, 122 seats for the 242-member House of Councilors), and has kept an alliance with the KOMEITO since the Abe administration started from December 2012. This alliance was formed because most LDP Diet members from both Houses found it difficult to win each constituency without the support from the KOMEITO.

This is why the LDP has currently adopted the KOMEITO's major policies, such as free education for children and private senior

Campaign speech at the 2019 unified local elections.

high school students, and university scholarships unnecessary to reimburse.

The LDP-KOMEITO ruling coalition has contributed to the political stability and produced long term economic growth, expansion of social welfare, education and so forth. It could be said that the conservative LDP has moved closer to center by partnering with the KOMEITO. The existence of the KOMEITO as a centrist party is extremely important for Japanese politics.

Campaign speech at the 2019 unified local elections.

The Relationship between the KOMEITO and China
(June 2019)

The most crucial issue in global politics now is undoubtedly how to face China, and especially, conflicts between the U.S. and China surrounding trade, technology and the South China Sea, which seems to be a struggle for hegemony.

China had lagged far behind Western Europe and Japan in industrialization and modernization. However, since the policy of "Economic Reform and Market Economy" started in 1978, China has tremendously developed and, as a result, has become the second largest nation by GDP, overtaking Japan.

By the way, Mr. Daisaku Ikeda who is the third president of the

Chinese delegation in front of the stone monument for Zhou Enlai, Kyoto City, 2019. Yuzuru TAKEUCHI, center, back row.

Chapter II The Liberal Democratic Party / The KOMEITO Ruling Coalition

religious organization, SOKA GAKKAI and the founder of the KOMEITO, first proposed the normalization of diplomatic relations between Japan and China for peace in East Asia in 1968, though the hostile atmosphere against Communism in the Cold War.

The KOMEITO had striven to work as a bridge between both nations through a close tie with the first Chinese Prime Minister Zhou Enlai, which culminated in the Japan-China Peace and Friendship treaty in 1978.

Therefore, the KOMEITO and China have constructed a firm relationship of mutual trust through interaction for the past four decades. I also visited China several times and sincerely discussed various kinds of themes with executives.

I understand the difficulty of resolving foreign issues between the

The Japan – China Parliamentary interaction conference, Beijing in 2009. Yuzuru TAKEUCHI, center.

U.S. and China. However, the U.S. should not excessively regard China with hostility, rather tenaciously continue insisting on worth of freedom, human rights democracy, multilateralism and international cooperation. China should also harmonize with international societies.

I hope both nations will reach compromises with each other and reach an agreement through patient negotiation. That is why the KOMEITO, having a strong connection with China, will be indispensable for world peace and happiness of human race.

Should we consider Modern Monetary Theory (MMT)?
(June 2019)

In the U.S. now, the most controversial economic and financial theme is an argument regarding Modern Monetary Theory (MMT). MMT is an economic theory proposing a new discipline for national finances in which a government should coordinate expenditure based on inflation rate instead of tax revenue.

The basic logic behind MMT is that no government defaults into bankruptcy due to national bonds dominated in its own currency. Therefore, it is nonsense for a government to curb its spending excessively concerning about bankruptcy. Therefore, a government need not adopt a primary balance that basic spending must be re-

Meeting with Prof. Stephanie Kelton on MMT, HR, July 2019. Yuzuru TAKEUCHI, left.

Plenary Session, HR, February, 2019.

strained within revenue every year.

There are a lot of critics against MMT both in the U.S. and Japan. For example, MMT is a heretical economic policy that allows expanding fiscal deficit, or a dangerous theory that secures funds by forcing a central bank print paper money.

However, MMT scholars argued against these critiques, saying most of them are misunderstandings. Discipline of finances for MMT is to avoid excessive inflation and deflation. Fiscal reconstruction policy has delayed recovery from deflation and conversely prompted it. Greece surely achieved a primary balance for their national finances, however, the economy collapsed.

MMT doesn't state that a government should expand debts unlimitedly, but rather points out excessive inflation, such as 3 – 4 % as an upper limit.

Given the Bank of Japan (BOJ) money easing policy of purchasing national bonds from banks and providing huge money to the private sector, it can be said that MMT has been partially implemented in Japan.

However, the Ministry of Finance (MOF) criticizes MMT and strongly insists on keeping the primary balance and the consumption tax rate hike from 8% to 10% on October 1st, 2019.

On the contrary, the MOF announced in an official statement on their website that any bonds dominated in its own currency from advanced nations such as Japan and the U.S. will never go into default. This is contradiction. Which one is right between MMT and the MOF?

Money easing policies under Abenomics have brought several results such as lowering unemployment rate and increasing corporate

Mr. Satoshi Fujii, Professor of Kyoto University (center), Mr. Shoji Nishida, Member of the HC (right), Yuzuru TAKEUCHI (left) discussed MMT, June, 2019.

profits, while raising the consumption tax rate from 5% to 8% led to a decline in real wagas and a delay in overcoming deflation.

It is indispensable for Japan to secure sources of revenues for various kinds of policies, such as social security, child raising, education, basic research of science, and so forth. Especially, it is an urgent matters to raise pay levels of those who work at care services and nursery schools.

I suppose we have to consider various possibilities of MMT without preconceptions or prejudice.

Japan should put more emphasis on Basic Scientific Research
(July 2019)

On October 1st 2018, Mr. Tasuku Honjo a special professor of Kyoto University, was awarded the Nobel Prize in Physiology or Medicine for his discovery of a protein that contributed to the development of an immunotherapeutic drug against cancer. Professor Honjo is the 27th Japanese Nobel Laureate, and for the category of natural science, the number of Japanese laureates is second only after the U.S. in the 21st century.

However, it is uncertain whether Japanese scientists can compete for the Nobel Prize hereafter. Currently, the budget for the basic research of science has been decreasing, which has led to a decline of Japanese scientists.

Professor Shinya Yamanaka, the director of the Center for iPS Cell Research and Application of Kyoto University was awarded the Nobel Prize in Physiology or Medicine in 2012 for his research on "induced pluripotent stem cells (iPS cells)". He worries that many high school and university students may not regard a scientist as an attractive job[i]. Actually, it has been said that the power of research and development in Japan has declined every year, which has resulted in a crisis for a science-led country.

Professor Honjo points out that the biggest issue in Japan is the depletion of scientific seeds which will reduce resources leading to future technology and invention. Innovation is merely a combination of technology, and is different from creation. The government needs to put further emphasis on the basic research of science to grow scientific seeds[ii].

I agree with what Professor Honjo said. Japan has developed as an industrial nation supported by science for 150 years. Therefore, the government should procure funds through various measures and allocate them to basic research of science prior to other policies.

Prof. Tasuku Honjo, Nobel Laureate in Physiology or Medicine, 2018.

---

i   June 2019 CHUOKORON p125
ii June 2019 CHUOKORON p125

Bitter dispute between Japan and South Korea, and Hong Kong Issue
(August 2019)

Regarding recent foreign affairs, a bitter dispute between Japan and South Korea has been escalating, namely South Korea's judicial decisions on wartime forced labor requiring Japanese enterprises to pay compensation, and Japan's decision to remove South Korea from the preferential trade list.

Japan insists its decision is due to national security concerns, however, South Korea claims Japan's decision is retaliation for political and historical grievances.

It seems to me that this feud fundamentally derives from different interpretations on the Treaty on Basic Relations between Japan and the Republic of Korea in 1965.

Given the details of the past negotiation between each country, and the principle of international laws, I don't believe that South Korea's judicial decision is legitimate.

It is merely a dodge that the government must have respect the decision of the Supreme Court due to separation of powers in South Korea. South Korea's government is undoubtedly responsible for the decision of the Supreme Court.

In accordance with the relevant agreement that the two countries concluded in 1965, the war time forced labor issue had been settled completely and finally.

Actually, the former South Korea's governments admitted that the wartime forced labor issue was included in the 1965 agreement.

If the interpretation of the 1965 Treaty is overturned by every change of government in South Korea, the stability and reliability of the relationship between the two countries can't be established or maintained.

On the other hand, Japan need to consider the victim consciousness of South Korea regarding Japan's past colonial period (1910-1945).

Even if bitter disputes remain between each government, mutual interactions by the private sector in various fields such as economy and culture, should be maintained. Both governments must not stir up hostility towards the other.

To conclude, each government needs to sincerely face each other to resolve this problem comprehensively.

With disabled persons in Laos, 2018. Yuzuru TAKEUCHI, center.

As for the problems in Hong Kong, I am concerned about the political impact. Ten years ago, some people worried about violations on the right of self-government and of human rights in the near future. I hope the Hong Kong government and its citizens try to reach an amicable settlement through dialogue.

In Japan, I will continue to do my best to realize a society that doesn't allow for any violation of human rights including domestic violence, sexual and power harassment, and so forth. Nobody should be excluded, and everybody must be included in our society.

With technical college students, Hanoi, Vietnam, 2018. Yuzuru TAKEUCHI, front row, third from the right.

Kyoto Imperial Palace.

Chapter III

The History of the KOMEITO

*Hear the people,
Fight for the people,
Stand with the people.*

Celebrating the New Year in Kimono, my home, Kyoto City, 2019.
Nishijin is my home town in Kyoto City and known for its production of kimono since the 15th century.

The History of the KOMEITO

The KOMEITO was founded by the SOKA GAKKAI, a religious organization in 1964 and at that time, the Liberal Democratic Party (LDP) was the ruling party. The LDP chiefly reflected the profit of capitalists while the biggest opposition party, the Social Democratic Party (SDP) was based on labor unions. At that time however, there were many people belonging to neither the capitalist class nor to labor unions. They were so called "the masses" and the KOMEITO was able to absorb these people.

At first the KOMEITO was mainly supported by the SOKA GAKKAI and gradually became supported by the people. The purpose of the KOMEITO was to pursue peace and happiness for both

The 2019 HC election rally, Kamigyo branch of the Kyoto Prefectural Headquarter of the KOMEITO.

individuals and humankind.

It's motto was: *For the people, Of the people, and By the people,* and it's political stance was centrist.

From the 1990s' the Japanese political landscape underwent a major transformation. In 1993, the Hosokawa administration was created by six opposition parties including the KOMEITO, which was the first change of government in the post war Japan. However, ten months later, the Hosokawa government abruptly collapsed and the LDP formed a ruling coalition with two other parties. The KOMEITO became an opposition party again.

In 1994, KOMEITO members of the House of Representatives joined the New Frontier Party (NFP), while the members of the House of Councilors, municipal and prefectural assembly members formed the *KOMEI Party.*

This transformation was in response to an era of two party-politics, the LDP and NFP. In 1994 the election system for the House of Representatives was reformed, which resulted in the introduction of single-seat constituencies. Due to this reform, several opposition parties joined the NFP.

However during the 1996 House of Representatives election, the NFP wasn't able to gain enough seats, which culminated in the disbanding of the NFP the following year. As a result, NFP members from the House of Representatives of the former KOMEITO and *KOMEI Party* established the NEW KOMEITO in 1998.

During the 1998 election for the House of Councilors, the DPJ performed well leaving the LDP without a majority. In 1999, to

Chapter III The History of the KOMEITO

prevent such a situation from occurring again, the LDP, Liberal Party and NEW KOMEITO agreed to partner in a coalition government. Soon after, the Liberal Party led by Ichiro Ozawa seceded from the coalition government leading to the first LDP-NEW KOMEITO coalition government in 2000.

The LDP-NEW KOMEITO ruling coalition had continued until the now defunct DPJ government (2009-2012), and restarted in the 2013 Abe administration as the LDP-NEW KOMEITO ruling coalition. The English name of the NEW KOMEITO was changed to the KOMEITO in 2014, commemorating the 50th anniversary of its foundation.

However, I consistently used "The KOMEITO" in this book in order to prevent readers from confusing.

Mrs. Kanae Yamamoto, candidate for the 2019 HC election.

Two election defeats made me grow as a statesman

I was born on June 25, 1958, in Kyoto City, Japan.

In 1971, I passed the entrance examination of St. Viator Rakusei Junior and Senior High School, one of the most prominent mission schools in Japan. When I was a first year student at the junior high school, I joined the school baseball club and until the third year of the senior high school, I had been recognized as an outstanding player on our team. During my senior high school days, our team went on to play in the quarterfinal game of Kyoto prefecture.

In 1978, I entered the law department of Kyoto University majoring in administrative law. However, I not only studied law, but also politics, history, sociology, literature, philosophy, economics, finance, science, and so on.

After graduation, I joined The Sanwa Bank, Ltd. (now The Mitsubishi UFJ Bank, Ltd.), as an executive trainee. I was engaged in various departments, for example: loans, analyzing the economic conditions, marketing, and large urban development. In 1990, I took office as acting director of the department of large urban developments.

In 1992, at 34 years of age, I was suddenly requested to run in the next general election for the KOMEITO. I was very surprised at this request and wavered whether to become a statesman or to succeed as a businessman.

Finally, I made up my mind to enter the political world, because

I found it important to work for public interest.

I was first elected as a Member of the House of Representatives in 1993 from the First District of Kyoto Prefecture under a multi-seat electoral system. During my first term, I belonged to the standing committee on financial affairs and was recognized as a promising and controversial statesman. However, in the 1996 general election, I failed to win a seat in the single-seat district which had been introduced in 1994.

In 1999, I was elected as a member of the Kyoto City Assembly, Kamigyo District of Kyoto City. At that time, there was nobody else that had switched from a member of the Diet to a local assembly member.

To tell the truth, it was hard for me. However, it was fairly difficult for the KOMEITO to win a seat in the single-seat constituency, and so I decided to train myself as a statesman from the local assembly. In 2003, I was subsequently reelected as a member of the Kyoto City Assembly.

In 2005, another chance had presented itself. I was requested to run for the general election again in the proportional representation system. However, I was defeated once again as a runner-up due to the LDP landslide victory by Prime Minister Koizumi's privatization of Japanese postal system.

I was really disappointed and exhausted, but I had no choice but to accept reality and move forward pursuing victory. I was determined to rise up and began to visit our supporters throughout my constituency, hearing people's voices and researching their potential needs for four years.

As a result, I was reelected as a Member of the House of Representatives in 2009. Thirteen years have passed since I lost my seat in the House of Representatives. To date, no other Diet Member except myself has made a comeback after 13 years.

While I had left the Diet for thirteen years, the book that encouraged me was "Representative Men of Japan" written by Mr. Kanzo Uchimura. This book is a biography of five great men and taught me how political leaders should be. I deeply regretted what I had done and made up my mind to become a statesman to contribute to the people. It is no exaggeration to say that two election defeats made me grow as a statesman.

I would like to express my profound gratitude to those who had supported me during my hard time.

The quarterfinal game of the high school baseball tournament, Kyoto Prefecture, 1976. I was a left-handed batter.

Profile

Yuzuru TAKEUCHI

Date of Birth: June 25, 1958
Birth Place: Kyoto Prefecture
Political Party: The KOMEITO
Member of the House of Representatives (5 terms)
Constituency:
    Kinki Proportional Representation Bloc

Education

March 1983	Faculty of Law, Kyoto University

Career

October 2019	Director of the Committee on Foreign Affairs, HR
October 2018	Secretary-general on Tax Commission of the KOMEITO
April 2018	Director of the Committee on Financial Affairs, HR
November 2017	Main members of the Taxation Council by the ruling coalition
October 2017	Elected as a Member of the House of Representatives (5th)
September 2016	Chairperson, Committee on Internal Affairs and Communication, HR
October 2015	The State Minister of Health, Labor and Welfare
December 2014	Elected as a Member of the House of Representatives (4th)
September 2014	Director of the House Steering Committee, HR
September 2014	The First Vice Chairperson on Diet Policy Committee of the KOMEITO
October 2013	Director of the Committee on Financial Affairs, HR
December 2012	Parliamentary Secretary for Finance (Abe Cabinet)

December 2012	Elected as a Member of the House of Representatives (3rd)
October 2010	Director of the Committee on Financial Affairs, HR
January 2010	Director of the Committee on Land, Infrastructure, Transport and Tourism, HR
October 2009	Chief Representative, the NEW KOMEITO Kyoto Prefectural Headquarters
August 2009	Director of the Special Committee on North Korea's abductions and other issues, HR
August 2009	Elected as a Member of the House of Representatives (2nd)
April 2003	Reelected as a Member of the Kyoto City Assembly
April 1999	Elected as a Member of the Kyoto City Assembly
July 1993	Elected as a Member of the House of Representatives (1st)
April 1983	Joined The Sanwa Bank Ltd. (The Bank of Mitsubishi UFJ, Ltd.)

HR = House of Representatives

Family

Wife, 2 children

My favarite book

"Representative Men of Japan / Japan and the Japanese" by Kanzo Uchimura

Hobbies

Baseball, Singing, Go (Strategic board game)

Japanese Politics
One Politician's Perspective
From the DPJ administration to the LDP-KOMEITO
ruling coalition (2010-2019)

2019年12月15日　初版第1刷発行

著　者　　Yuzuru TAKEUCHI
発行者　　瓜谷　綱延
発行所　　株式会社文芸社
　　　　　〒160-0022　東京都新宿区新宿1－10－1
　　　　　　　　　電話　03-5369-3060（代表）
　　　　　　　　　　　　03-5369-2299（販売）

印刷所　　図書印刷株式会社

© Yuzuru TAKEUCHI 2019 Printed in Japan
乱丁本・落丁本はお手数ですが小社販売部宛にお送りください。
送料小社負担にてお取り替えいたします。
本書の一部、あるいは全部を無断で複写・複製・転載・放映、データ配信する
ことは、法律で認められた場合を除き、著作権の侵害となります。
ISBN978-4-286-21162-6